PIANO • VOCAL • GUITAR

WAIT FOR ME THE BEST FROM
REBECCA ST. JAMES

CONTENTS

ISBN 0-634-06409-6

HAL•LEONARD®
CORPORATION
7777 W. BLUEMOUND RD. P.O. BOX 13819 MILWAUKEE, WI 53213

Visit Hal Leonard Online at
www.halleonard.com

EXPRESSIONS OF YOUR LOVE

Words and Music by REBECCA ST. JAMES,
MATT BRONLEEWE, CHRIS TOMLIN
and JESSE REEVES

WAIT FOR ME

Words and Music by
REBECCA ST. JAMES

Dar-ling, did you know that I,___ I dream a-bout___ you? Wait-ing for the look in your

Cm7 Bb(add4)

eyes when we meet ___ for the first time. ___

Eb Bb(add4)/D

Dar - ling, did you know that I, ___ I pray a - bout ___ you? Pray - ing that you ___ will hold

Ab(add2) Bbsus Bb

on. Keep your lov - ing eyes on - ly for me. 'Cause I am

Eb Bb(add4}

wait - ing for, pray - ing for ___ you, dar - ling. ___ Wait for me, ___

Dar - ling, did you know I dream __ a - bout life to -

geth - er, know - ing it will be for - ev - er? __ I'll be yours __

__ and you'll __ be mine. __ And dar - ling, when I say, "'Til death __ do us

part," I'll mean it with all __ of my heart. Now and al - ways

I THANK YOU

Words and Music by REBECCA ST. JAMES,
MARC BYRD, LINDA ELIAS
and STEVE HINDALONG

ting go, _____ nev-er __ let-ting go. __

Some-thing stirred __ in-side __ me, __

some-thing I just can't de-ny, __ for You have healed __

__ my spir-it; __ Your mer-cy has re-stored my life. __

GOD

Words and Music by REBECCA ST. JAMES
and TEDD TJORNHOM

LAMB OF GOD

Words and Music by REBECCA ST. JAMES,
MATT BRONLEEWE and JEREMY ASH

GO AND SIN NO MORE

Words and Music by REBECCA ST. JAMES,
TEDD TJORNHOM and MICHAEL ANDERSON

A CRADLE PRAYER

Words and Music by REBECCA ST. JAMES
and CHARLES GARRETT

PRAY

Words and Music by REBECCA ST. JAMES,
MICHAEL QUINLAN and TEDD TJORNHOM

Slowly, very freely

Moderately fast

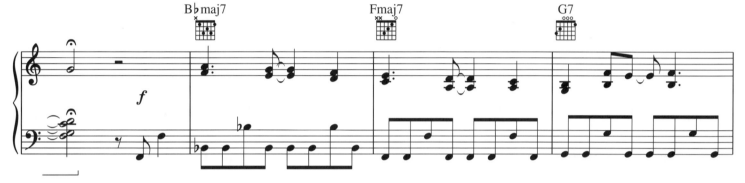

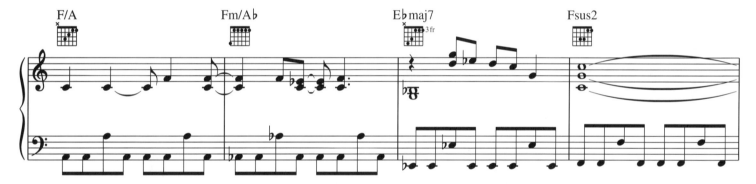

Je- sus, I am brok-en now.__ Be-fore__

* Vocal line written one octave higher than sung

Original key: D♭ major. This edition has been transposed down one half-step to be more playable.

MIRROR

Words and Music by REBECCA ST. JAMES
and TEDD TJORNHOM

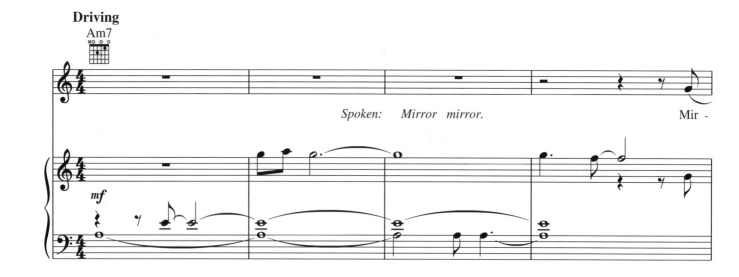

YES, I BELIEVE IN GOD

Words and Music by REBECCA ST. JAMES
and JANET FOLGER

HERE I AM

Words and Music by REBECCA ST. JAMES,
BILL DEATON and ERIC CHAMPION

STAND

Words and Music by REBECCA ST. JAMES
and REGIE HAMM

REBORN

Words and Music by REBECCA ST. JAMES
and MATT BRONLEEWE

SPEAK TO ME

Words and Music by REBECCA ST. JAMES,
TEDD TJORNHOM and JOSH DEATON

BREATHE

Words and Music by
MARIE BARNETT

Moderately slow

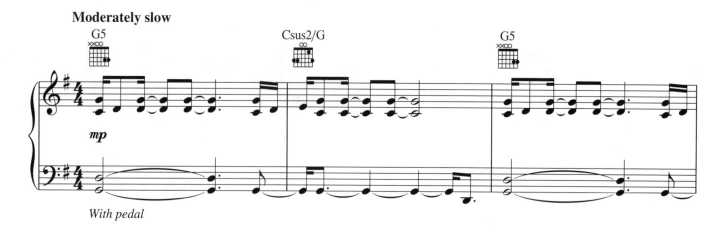

With pedal

This is __ the air __ I breathe, __

this is __ the air __ I breathe, __ Your ho - ly pres-

Original key: G♭ major. This edition has been transposed up one half-step to be more playable.

SONG OF LOVE

Words and Music by REBECCA ST. JAMES,
MATT BRONLEEWE and JEREMY ASH

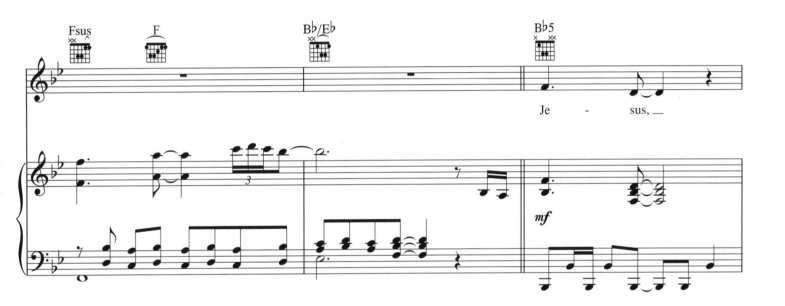

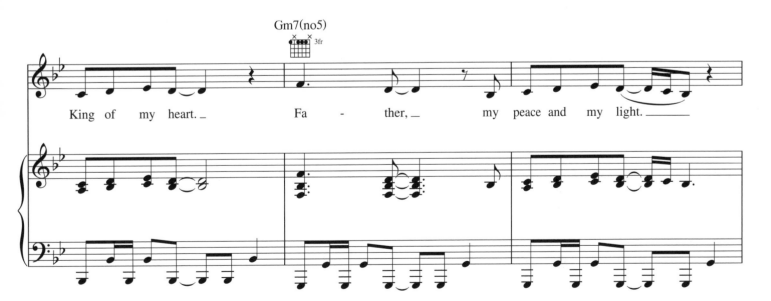

Original key: B major. This edition has been transposed down one half-step to be more playable.

YOUR LOVE BROKE THROUGH

Words and Music by KEITH GREEN,
TODD FISHKIND and RANDY STONEHILL

PSALM 139

Words and Music by
REBECCA ST. JAMES